AN
EASY-READ
FACT
BOOK

Comets

Martyn Hamer

Franklin Watts

London   New York   Toronto   Sydney

©1984 Franklin Watts Ltd

First published in Great Britain
    1984 by
Franklin Watts Ltd
12a Golden Square
London W1

First published in the USA by
Franklin Watts Inc.
387 Park Avenue South
New York
N.Y. 10016

UK ISBN: 0 86313 167 0
US ISBN: 0-531-03779-7
Library of Congress Catalog Card
    Number 83-51585

Designed and produced by
David Jefferis

Illustrated by
Eagle Artists
Hayward Art Group
Christopher Forsey
Michael Roffe

Photographs supplied by
Mary Evans Picture Library
Science Photo Library

Technical Consultant
Iain Nicholson BSc, FRAS

Printed in Great Britain by
    Cambus Litho, East Kilbride

AN
EASY-READ
FACT
BOOK

Comets

Contents

⑤

②

①

"Dirty snowballs"

A comet is a frozen mixture of ice, dust
and rock — a giant dirty "snowball"
moving through the depths of space.

Sometimes this snowball, called the
nucleus, passes near the Sun. Then the
Sun's rays start to melt the icy mass.
Soon the nucleus is surrounded by a

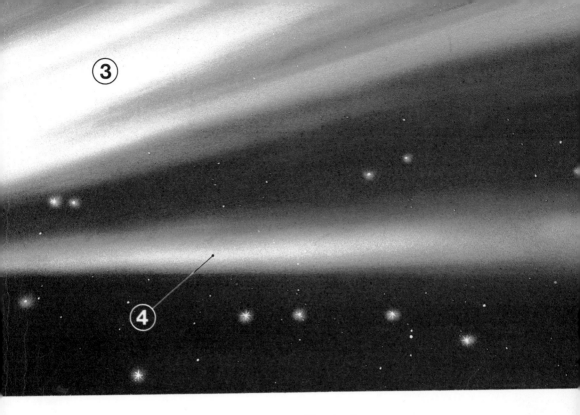

thin cloud of gas and dust, called the coma. More gas and dust particles may stretch back, away from the Sun, to form a long glowing tail. In fact, the tail is usually made up of a *pair* of tails — one of gas, one of dust. It is not common for a tail of any sort to be visible from Earth.

Although comet tails may be millions of miles long, there is barely enough material in them to fill a large suitcase!

△Here you can see a big comet compared to the Earth in size.
1 Nucleus — the "snowball," too small to be seen at this scale. May be anything up to 31 miles (50 km) across.
2 Coma, or "head" of comet
3 Gas tail
4 Dust tail
5 Earth to scale

5

In the beginning

Where do comets come from? Scientists think they are matter left over when the Solar System formed nearly five billion years ago.

Then, the Solar System (the name given to the Sun and its family of worlds) was nothing but a huge whirling cloud of dust and gases. The material in the middle of the cloud formed the Sun. Further out, the planets and their moons formed.

The comet cloud lies beyond the planets, between Earth and the nearest stars. It is a vast globe of waste material. Billions of chunks of ice and rock move silently in space.

Occasionally, a comet drifts in toward the Sun and loops around it at high speed.

Once past the Sun, the comet heads back into outer space and disappears again.

▷These pictures show the way in which many scientists think the Solar System was formed.
Top Five billion years ago, a vast cloud of gas and dust swirled in space.
Middle The material in the cloud joined together to form the Sun and planets.
Bottom The Solar System today, with Sun, nine planets and many moons. Comets sometimes loop through the Solar System.

Wanderers in space

Comets have been spotted throughout history. One of the few comets which has kept on coming back is Halley's comet. One of the early sightings was in 1066. The event is recorded on the Bayeux Tapestry, a huge woven picture story of the Norman conquest.

Donati's comet, seen in 1858, was thought to be the most beautiful ever, with gas and dust tails streaming across the sky.

△Here is a small part of the Bayeux Tapestry. Halley's comet is shown at the top, above the English king, Harold. Comets were often thought to bring doom. In Harold's case, this was true — he was killed the same year at the Battle of Hastings.

▷This picture was drawn over a century ago and shows Donati's comet.

8

Types of comet

▽Here you see the
orbits of the planets.
From the Sun outward,
they are: Mercury,
Venus, Earth, Mars,
Jupiter, Saturn, Uranus,
Neptune, Pluto.
   Also shown are
long-period comet
orbits (yellow line).
Shorter period orbits are
shown in red and green.

Comets are divided up according to the length of their periods. A comet's period is the length of time it takes to complete one orbit. An orbit is the curving path which planets and comets take as they move around the Sun. The orbits of the planets are nearly circular, while those of comets are long, sweeping ovals.

"Short-period" comets rarely move out further than the giant planet Jupiter. These comets have periods ranging from 3.3 to 60 years. Longer short-period comets go out as far as Neptune or Pluto. They can have periods of up to 200 years.

"Long-period" comets go far beyond the planets. At the furthest point in its orbit, such a comet may be over 5.5 trillion miles (9 trillion km) from the Sun. For comparison, the Earth is only 93 million miles (150 million km) from the Sun.

▽This picture shows a comet as it swings around the Sun.
1 Comet is still a frozen mass of ice, dust and gas.
2 Coma grows around nucleus as Sun's heat melts ices.
3, 4 Tail grows.
5 Comet moves away from Sun.
6, 7 Tail fades as Sun's rays get weaker. Once again frozen and dark, the comet nucleus moves into outer space.

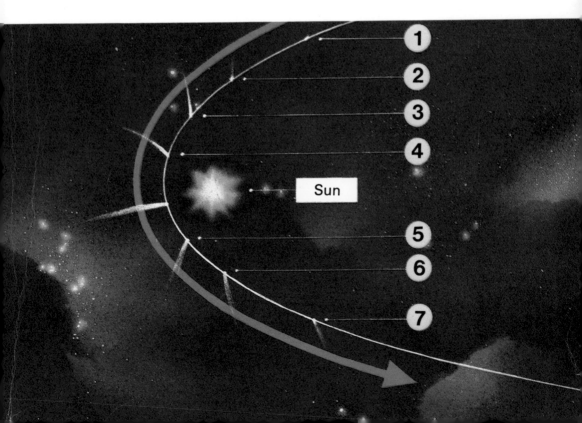

Halley's comet

This is the most famous comet of all. It was named after Edmund Halley, an English astronomer, who lived over 200 years ago. He predicted the comet's return in 1759. Nowadays all comets are named after the person who spots them first. In fact, if you

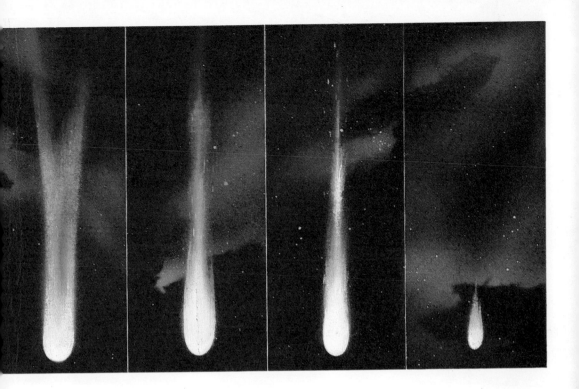

managed to spot a new one some dark night, it would have *your* name!

Halley's comet was last seen in 1910. Cameras and telescopes were focused on the spectacular visitor. The picture sequence above is based on a set of photographs taken then. You can clearly see how the tail grows from nothing. At perihelion, the closest approach to the Sun, the tail is at its biggest. Then it rapidly fades as the comet speeds away from the Sun.

△Halley's comet, growing and shrinking, during its appearance of 1910.

Halley saw a great comet in 1682. He made records of comets that had followed the same pathway in the past. This was how he predicted that the comet would reappear close to 1759.

Swing around the Sun

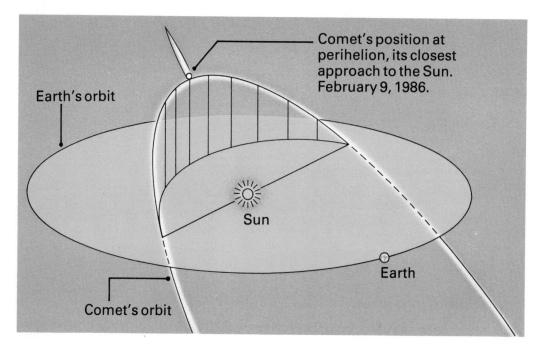

Comet's position at perihelion, its closest approach to the Sun. February 9, 1986.

Earth's orbit

Sun

Earth

Comet's orbit

△ This diagram shows the positions of Earth and Halley's comet on February 9, 1986. To give an idea of scale, the distance between Earth and Sun is about 93 million miles (150 million km).

The Earth, like most of the other planets, goes around the Sun in a more-or-less circular orbit. As the diagram above shows, Halley's comet approaches the Sun at a steep angle. It will be on the far side of the Sun when it is at perihelion.

In 1910, the only recording instruments were eyes and cameras. Now, a huge range of instruments can be used. Computers can even improve the

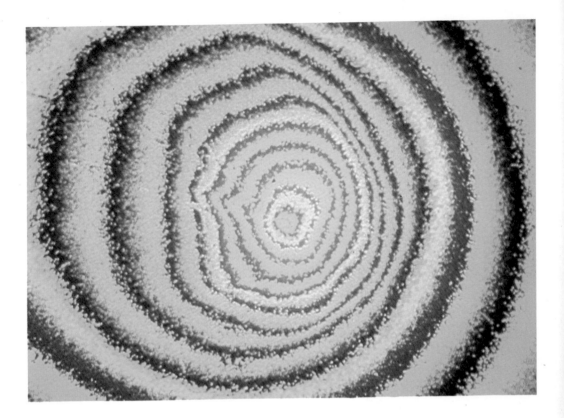

results from photographs taken in 1910.

The picture above shows the results of computer enhancement. The bright colors are coded to show parts of the comet which would otherwise be invisible. No one in 1910 could have spotted the small "nick" near the nucleus. This was probably a jet of material blowing out from the middle of the comet.

△ This is a computer-image, based on a photograph taken in 1910. You can clearly see the small "nick," a jet of material breaking away from the nucleus.

Space probes to Halley's comet

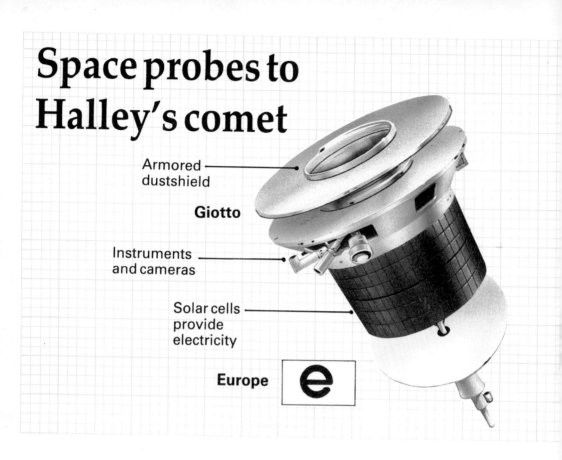

Armored dustshield

Giotto

Instruments and cameras

Solar cells provide electricity

Europe

△ These spaceprobes are being built to get close-up information about Halley's comet.

Four spaceprobes from Earth will visit Halley's comet in 1986.

Europe's *Giotto* is named after an Italian painter who saw the comet in 1301. The probe will carry cameras, dust detectors and other instruments. It should pass within 311 miles (500 km) of the comet. To protect the instruments from the dust and gas particles of the comet, *Giotto* has a

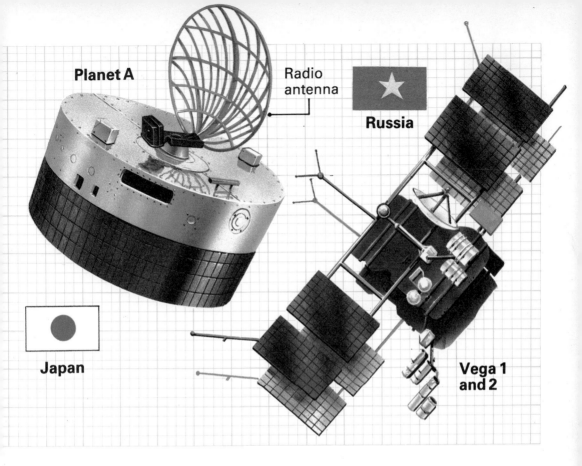

Planet A

Radio antenna

Russia

Japan

Vega 1 and 2

sheet of armor-plate on the front.

Planet A is Japan's spaceprobe. Instruments aboard will take pictures of the coma.

Russia's two identical probes are called *Vega 1* and *2*. After launch, they will first go to the planet Venus. Then they will swing on toward Halley's comet, where they will take pictures and measurements.

△ Vega 1 and 2 will launch capsules to Venus before they pass the comet.

Other comets

△ This is Arend-Roland, a comet which appeared in 1957. The spike is rock and dust along the line of the comet's orbit, lit by the glow of Arend-Roland itself.

The regular appearance of some comets can be predicted, but most appear as unexpected visitors in the sky. This is because their orbits are so big that they may take thousands of years to return. And, quite simply, there were no astronomers to record their last appearance.

Several new comets are discovered each year. You can see some recent ones on these pages. A few are bright enough to see unaided, but most are faint, fuzzy objects which can be seen only with powerful telescopes.

Some of the most exciting recent discoveries (including the first sighting of Halley's comet in 1983) have been made by the IRAS satellite. IRAS (Infra-Red Astronomy Satellite) is a very sensitive detector of sources of heat in the sky. Although a comet is icy-cold in outer space, it is still a little warmer than the space around it.

△In 1983, comet
IRAS-Araki-Alcock made
the closest approach of a
comet to Earth since
1770. In this picture,
special filters have
turned the stars red and
green. They appear as
streaks because of the
long time-exposure
used with the camera.

▷This heat image of the
comet was taken by the
IRAS satellite. Red zones
are warmest.

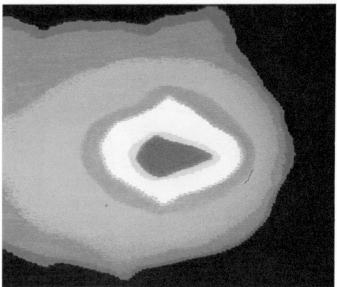

Sun-grazers

Some comets make very close approaches to the Sun, perhaps within 621,000 miles (1 million km) or less. They are called Sun-grazers, and may never survive the brief trip around the Sun's fiery surface.

The Sun's heat vaporizes the ices of a comet at a furious rate. Smaller comets may break up and fall apart, never to be seen again. Others may simply fall into the Sun. But the speed at which a comet travels past the Sun is so great that bigger comets can survive the trip. After a few passes, the remains of such a comet may look like a chunk of burned cinder, all its ices long since boiled away.

The picture opposite shows what a nightmare ride on a large Sun-grazer might be like. The Sun itself is below the horizon of this 31 mile (50 km) mini-world, but huge flares leap out into space.

▷This is what you might see if you were standing on the surface of a comet nucleus as it passed close to the Sun. Huge explosions of flaming gas — solar flares — burst across the sky.

Back to the depths of space

△This comet is seen as it moves away from the Sun. Its tail will soon fade and disappear. It is shown here as if seen from beyond the Moon. The crescents of Earth and Moon can be seen on the right.

Once past perihelion, many comets go so far into space that they will not return for thousands of years. One such is Kohoutek's comet, last seen in 1973. Its next appearance is not due for another 75,000 years.

The comet cloud is about 50,000 times further from the Sun than the Earth. Temperatures are low enough to freeze the ices of a comet hard as steel. There is little light. From this

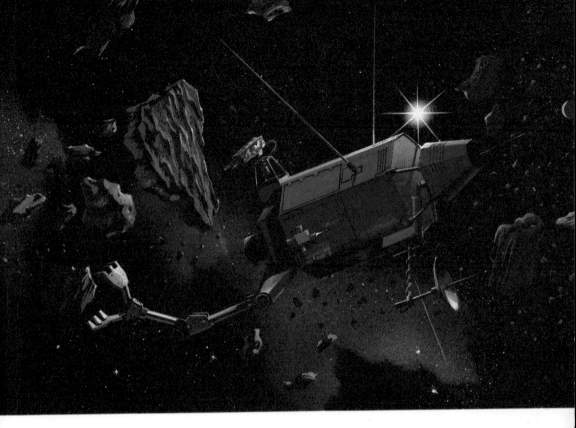

distance, the Sun appears no more than a very bright star.

In the future scientists may wish to capture pieces of a comet. So a comet-sampler spaceprobe could be built. The probe would gently close in on a comet nucleus. Robot grippers would grasp chunks of material, placing them carefully in specimen tanks. Then the probe would blast for Earth and the research teams waiting there.

△Soon we may be able to send out probes to bring back comet samples. Here an explorer-probe collects samples near Jupiter.

Comet-crash!

In 1983, comet IRAS-Araki-Alcock passed within 3 million miles (4.8 million km) of Earth. This seems a long way, but it is not far by Solar System standards. The Earth is bombarded daily by all sorts of cosmic matter and has passed through a comet tail more than once. So a strike by a comet is unlikely but not impossible.

What would happen if a comet-crash occurred? The answer depends on the size of the pieces. Smaller chunks would burn up as they came through the atmosphere, but larger pieces could survive to hit the Earth. A really big strike would be like the explosion of many H-bombs. If it splashed down in an ocean, tidal waves would swamp coastal areas. Boiling steam would shoot into the air and cover much of the world in dense cloud. This would cut off the Sun, perhaps starting a new ice age.

▷This is going to be a *very* near miss! Lots of small chunks of comet will hit the Earth in a few minutes. However, the main nucleus will just miss.

Some scientists think a small comet may have exploded in Siberia in 1908. Then a mystery blast flattened trees for many miles.

Comet watching

△A family trip out to the country is a great idea for comet-watchers. Don't forget warm clothes and folding chairs.

Halley's comet should be the most spectacular sight of the winter and spring of 1985–6. To see it at its best, you will need to get away from the city. Street lamps brighten the skies, making a good view impossible.

Why not get a group together to go out into the country to see the comet at its finest? It will be closest to Earth on April 11, 1986, at a distance of about 39 million miles (63 million km). It

should be a glorious sight with its tail streaming out before it.

To record the event, you can use any camera which has a "B" setting. This lets you keep the shutter open as long as you like. Use a color slide film, such as Ektachrome 200, and try exposures of between one and four minutes. The longer exposure gives more detail. But you will need a support to keep the camera steady.

△Camera, binoculars and a small telescope, if you have one, are all the equipment you need. A tripod is the best support for telescope and camera. It will keep the picture really steady.

Meteor showers

△Meteors appear to come from roughly the same part of the sky. This is called the radiant. You are unlikely to see several at the same time, but you might be lucky.

Another activity is meteor-spotting. Meteors are small bits of space matter which are seen as streaks of light or "falling stars." They hit the atmosphere at anything up to 45 miles/second (72 km/second), and burn up by air friction, causing the glowing streak in the sky.

Meteors often come in "showers" over a period of several nights. Many are thought to be the remains of long-dead comets, moving in meteor

Meteor showers to spot

Name of shower	Date of biggest display	Number seen in an hour	Associated comet
Lyrids	April 21	5	186 II
Eta Aquarids	May 4	20	Halley
Perseids	August 12	40	186 III
Draconids	October 10	Varies	Giacobini-Zinner
Orionids	October 21	15	Halley
Taurids	November 1	5	Encke
Andromedids	November 14	Just a few	Biela
Leonids	November 17	10	Temple
Ursids	December 22	5	Tuttle

streams across the Solar System. Every now and then, we pass through such a stream. This is when you may see a meteor shower.

The chart above lists nine showers you can look out for. The showers are named after the constellation or star group from which they seem to come. Check the position of the constellation in an astronomy book and face that way, watching and waiting. Good luck!

△This chart shows comet-linked meteor showers. The numbers seen in an hour are likely to be the most you will see. Expect fewer and you will not be disappointed.

Glossary

Here is a list of some of the technical words used in this book.

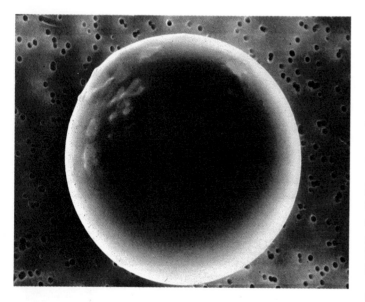

△ What do bits of comet look like? This odd picture gives you the answer. It is thought to be a tiny speck of comet dust. It is magnified over 2,000 times. Find out how it was collected on the opposite page.

Atmosphere
The blanket of air around the Earth which we breathe. Other planets have atmospheres, but of different gas mixtures.

Coma
The "mini-atmosphere" of gas and dust which surrounds a comet when the Sun's heat melts the nucleus.

Constellation
Group of stars which form a pattern in the sky. There are 88 constellations.

Nucleus
The solid core of a comet. Thought to be a dirty snowball of frozen ice, gas, dust and rock.

Orbit
The curving path in space which a small object takes around a larger one. Comet orbits are long ovals which go far out into space, often beyond Neptune and Pluto.

Perihelion
Closest point of a comet's orbit to the Sun. Aphelion is the point furthest away from the Sun.

Period
The length of time a comet takes to complete one orbit.

Solar flare
Explosion of hot gas from the surface of the Sun.

Vaporize
Frozen ice turning into a vapor or gas.

Comet facts

Here are some interesting facts about comets.

△Sometimes a comet nucleus splits in two. You can see such a crumbling break-up in the picture above. The two pieces may split up completely or become twin comets.

The word comet comes from the Greek *kometes.* It means "long-haired" star.

Halley's comet was seen as long ago as 240 BC. Edmund Halley was the first to predict its return. The Eta Aquarid and Orionid meteor showers are both linked to the comet. They follow its orbital path, but at different points.

A comet's period is not exact. It often varies if a comet is swung off-course by a close pass to a planet. Edmund Halley's prediction was not quite right because of this. He thought the comet would appear in 1757 but it actually arrived two years later.

Short-period comets are frequent visitors. Encke's comet has the shortest period known — just 3.3 years.

When a comet approaches the Sun, its tail streams behind it. When it is going away from the Sun, the tail goes in front of it. It is blown forward by the pressure of the Sun's radiation.

High-flying planes have been sent up to capture samples of comet dust. Once over 60,000 ft (18,000 m) the plane is above any air pollution and the pilot can open small sticky plates below the wings. Some dust samples are volcanic ash or remains of rocket exhaust. But some come from space and are probably bits of comet.

Index

DATE DUE			